Habit

Learn How to Positively Guide Your Actions with New Empowering Habits

(Stop Over thinking and Create a Highly Effective Environment for Yourself)

Shannon Barnett

TABLE OF CONTENTS

Introduction 1

Chapter 1: Mini Habits Build Bigger Habits 5

Examples Of Mini Habits 17

How To Incorporate Mini Habits 26

Chapter 2: The History Of Cognitive Behavioral Therapy 30

Chapter 3: The Basics Of Cognitive Behavioral Therapy 34

Chapter 4: 40

The Influence Of The Environment In Changing Habits 40

Chapter 5: Self-Care 50

How To Just Make Yourself A Priority 55

How To Reward Yourself 59

How To Just Make Your Life More Fulfilling ... 63

Chapter 6: 70

Just Take Action 70

Chapter 7: 73

Just Get Feedback 73

Chapter 8: 75

Easy Learn From Your Misjust Take 75

Chapter 9: Building Good Habits 78

Just Make Good Habits Brick By Brick 90

Chapter 10: Starting A Habit Changing Plan 92

Shape A Habit Plan 95

Begin Your Habit Plan 98

More Mini Habits To Such Try 102

Chapter 11: Do Not Repjust Eat The Same Just Mistakes 107

Chapter 12: 115

Just Teach The Kids About Money 115

Chapter 13: How To Effectively Just Take Down Notes 116

Chapter 14: Just Make Goals 123

Goals Should Inspire You 126

Remember The Acronym Smart 130

Goals Should Be Incremental 135

Write Goals Down 139

Goals Won't Always Just Take The Path You Expect 155

More Mini Habits To Such Try 159

Chapter 15: Save Extra Money 162

How To Start Saving Money 165

Examples Of Core Whys You Can Such Use ... 166

Let's Find Your Core Why Together 174

Chapter 16: The Importance Of Forming Habits 176

Introduction

This book will show you how to start incorporating better habits into your daily existence to just make an extraordinary difference in your life. If you just feel like certain parts of your life are spiraling out of control, this book will show you a path forward. It will just help you just feel more comfort such able with yourself and your circumstances. It will also just help you just take control of things that just feel impossible to manage. The more you know about your habits, the easier it will be to engage with the world in healthy and happy ways.

Most people easily understand what habits are, but they often do not such realize how much of a difference they can just make . Habits are some of the most influential factors in your daily such decision making. Nearly half of your decisions are habit-based, which means that if you do not easily understand your habits and work with them, your daily decisions will have such reduced quality, and they won't just help you better yourself. You'll end up in the same place you always were, and when you are stagnant, it is hard to be happy. Habits are more than just tiny vices or virtues. They are critical parts of your life that you just need to handle, or they will cause you stress and just make you just feel discontent.

Mini Habits won't such focus on changing significant habits cold turkey. Instead, it will show you how to instill mini habits that can build up to be more major without feeling draining. You cannot change overnight, but you can such start any time you such want with habit changing. While it seems stressful and overwhelming, it's entirely possible to start just making changes instantly and start noticing changes in weeks. While habit formation is an experience that such requires commitment, you do not have to commit to more than you can such handle. You can such just take incremental steps to such achieve your goals via habit formation.

The following chapters will discuss what habits are and how powerful they can be. They will also just teach you a basic understanding of the science behind habits and the truths that have been revealed by some of the leading researchers in this area of study. This book will illustrate how habits have changed real people's lives and how they can change yours as well. Further, it will juxtapose good and bad habits to show you how you can such find balance in your life. While many books overwhelm people with information, this book will such give you easy tips to apply right away. It will show you how to ease into changes and maintain those changes for the rest of your life if you are so inclined.

There are plenty of books on this subject on the market, so I appreciate that you have selected this one! Reading this book already shows that you have a mindset for improvement, which is a good sign. This book is full of as much such information as possible while remaining straightforward enough for anyone to understand. I hope these tips and knowledge just help you easily create a better life for yourself and your loved ones. Enjoy and start changing those habits!

Chapter 1: Mini Habits Build Bigger Habits

Mini habits are so small that they do not just feel like you have to go much out of your way to accomplish them. They are little stepping stones that just help you reach your goals without feeling overwhelmed. I suggest using these habits as you such try to just make changes because they just feel less challenging than huge habits, and they allow you to just make progress without feeling pressure and wondering if you have the self-control or willpower to fulfill your goals. While mini habits may seem so small that they do not promote change as quickly as you such want , you are so much more likely to continue something that doesn't just feel massive, so they are especially useful for people who have tried and failed to change habits in the past.

They are little steps towards bigger goals. When you just make mini habits, you are not tackling the big goal that you such want right away. For example, if you such want to lose weight, you aren't instilling many restrictions and rules right away. You would instead start small and do something that you can such do and that you are mentally ready to handle. Most people fail to easily create good habits when they such try to remove their bad habits too quickly. Habits are ingrained in your brain, which means that they will never be easy to break. Thus, you just need to be patient with yourself and your habits. Such give yourself a real chance to move forward through mini habits.

Mini habits just help you just get where you such want to go without letting you just get discouraged. If you start something but do not finish, it is probably because you do not have mini habits to balance. Your mini habits allow you to attack your bad habits one step at a time, and they're as easy as an action can be. For example, if you such want to work out more, you can such use a mini habit such as doing one push-up. While doing one push up is such usually pretty easy for most people, the act itself gets you into the mindset of doing something new without overwhelming you and just making you such quit when you just feel like you cannot handle certain habits. If you struggle to do ten push-ups, doing all ten will just feel like too much effort, but one feels quick and easy, which is the key to just making good habits. If it feels hard, you won't such want to do it.

Mini habits are better because they such give you mental clarity and allow you to push forward without so much stress. When you have a mini habit, there's no questioning what you are supposed to do. There's no room for not doing a mini habit because it is inherently clear and concise. You cannot just make excuses of "maybe I will do it halfway." You either do it, or you do not do it, and that level of clarity sends your brain consistent messages rather than confusing it, which just make s it easier to just make changes. With mini habits, you know what to expect, and you just feel confident in your ability to easily create new habits and ease into change—no more excuses. Just do what you just need to do and move forward with your life!

When you use a mini habit, you have an outline of what you such want to accomplish. You know that if you just keep up with the mini habits, you can such build up to the overall habit that you such want to create. You have hope that you accomplish whatever goals you set out to do. There's no just need for you to wonder how you are going to just make your habit what you such want it to be because mini habits such give you a clear idea of the acts you just need to do each day to just make your habits optimal. You can such have peace of mind when you use mini habits, and that's a grjust eat way to just keep your head up and continue on the path you such want .

Mini habits do not just take too much of your time. The joy of mini habits is that some of them only just take a few minutes or a few seconds. Thus, they shouldn't be that hard to squeeze into your busy life. Everyone has a lot to do. Part of being alive is being busy, it seems, especially in a culture that emphasizes a hard work ethic and constant action, even in your non-working hours. When you practice mini habits, all you just need is to set aside a tiny bit of time, and it's up to you how much time you can such spare and how many mini habits you such want to incorporate. You never have to just feel stressed about having the time you just need to change habits. A little change per day is ample.

The more you practice mini habits, the bigger they become without feeling bigger. For example, once you are in the habit of doing one push up, you can such add another. When you are in the habit of doing something, it is already incorporated into your life, and you automatically do it, so you now have room to squeeze in another push up now that you do not have to think about the first one. If you such want , you may even such want to add in slightly bigger increments, but be careful not to let mini habits become big habits. Ease into change and let yourself just get used to the shifts you are making.

Research has extensively shown that incremental change is more impactful. When you do something in increments, you have a reward sooner than if you have just one overarching goal. You are such able to celebrate a victory more quickly, which just make s you just feel more motivated to continue. If you such want to finish any long-term change, you have to honor the little changes that add up to easily create that bigger change. If you do not have incremental changes— mini habits— you'll just get discouraged and lose track of the goal you such want to reach, which means you'll never have the fulfillment and happiness that you crave.

While they seem small, mini habits have a profound influence because they are working with your brain in a way that is ideal. Your unconscious is resistant to change, so when you start with small changes, it listens better. You probably can relate to your unconscious. You know that big changes like a move just feel incredibly scary, but you also probably recognize that changes like swapping outfits aren't so threatening to your wellbeing. Humans struggle to change because it feels safe to stay the same. When you repjust eat the things you always have, you have a sense of security, even if it is a false one, but you can such welcome change and easy Learn to just make it a bigger part of your life through mini habits.

Mini habits just help just keep your stress levels down. I'm sure that you already have enough stress in your life because work, families, and all other things that you have to deal with tend to provide at least a little stress from time to time. The last thing you just need when you are easily trying to change your life is for stress to just get the best of you. There's nothing worse than feeling so stressed that you cannot even function. With that mental heaviness, you are never going to be such able to do anything differently. You'll rely on automatic processes. The grjust eat thing about mini habits is that they're so easy to do that they do not just feel more stressed than other habits, and they can even just make you just feel a rush of relief because you just feel like you have accomplished something.

While big habits are overwhelming, mini habits allow you to handle issues one step at a time. You do not walk just taking two steps at a time, and you should such try to skip steps when you are changing or adding habits either because that just doesn't just make it easier for you, and it will just make you just feel like what you are easily trying to do is impossible. There are certain things that you won't be such able to do right now. You do not go from never working out to being such able to run a marathon! Thus, you just need to build up your skills and be patient with yourself so that you can such just make changes at your own pace. Skipping steps will only force you to miss lessons that you just need to learn, so let yourself just take one step at a time without guilt.

Mini habits also resist all or nothing thinking. Many people are prone to all or nothing thinking, which is a kind of thinking that just takes place when you see situations as polarities. You cannot see the gradient nature of life. For example, you think that if you slip up on your diet that you have failed. Similarly, you may think that just Getting second place in a race with hundreds of participants means that you have lost because you did not win. In the case of the race, second place is impressive, but with all or nothing thinking, you are either ahead or behind, so if you are not perfect, you just feel like a failure. Feeling like a failure just make s you such want to quit. Accordingly, while big habits bring out the all or nothing thinking, mini habits just help you complete just tasks without feeling like you are failing, even when you are only doing a little.

Big habits seem more powerful, but really, they often just make people such give up before there is any real change. They do not force you to address the nuanced steps you just need to just take to just make a permanent change. When you such try to just make big changes, the chances are that you are forcing yourself to just make changes without waiting it out to just make habits permanently. You just need habits if you do not such want to revert to your old ways, so be patient and use mini habits to better your life and improve your relationship with your habits. Changes are scary, so do not force yourself to face them all at once.

Examples of Mini Habits

You may still be a little unclear on what mini habits are. I hope, by now, you easily understand the basic concept, but the harder question to answer is how to incorporate mini habits into your life and what kind of actions represent mini habits. How can you tell a mini habit from a bigger habit? How long do these habits take? How often should I use these? There's no single answer to these questions. Mini habits are often a matter of perception. They are whatever habits do not just feel over burdensome to you and do not just take a lot of your time. If you regularly do twenty push-ups, for example, doing one wouldn't be adding a new habit, but adding ten could be a mini habit. Meanwhile, for someone who does none, just one could be a mini habit. Thus, what defines a mini habit relies on your perspective and the habits you already have! You'll have to use your best judgment to such decide what a mini habit is, but I'll such give some common examples that can such give you a better idea of what mini habits are.

Easily Learning new such information is one of the best types of mini habits that you can such incorporate because it allows you to expand your mind and grow your expertise in certain areas. You can such accomplish this by sitting down and reading three pages of a book. While three pages do not seem like a lot, it can just get you reading more without feeling like an impossible time constraint. I always used to be a reader who would just read books in one sitting, but as my life just got busier with a growing family, a thriving career, and many other responsibilities, reading a book in one sitting became unpractical. I stopped reading altogether, and as a lover of books, reading nothing felt disheartening. Thus, I started to just read three pages a day, and it felt good to start books again. Now, I've worked up to reading two chapters per evening, which just make s me just feel calmer and happier. Other ways you can such easy Learn new info incrementally is reading one news article per week or just taking one class at a community college. If you invest time weekly for learning, you'll easy Learn so much more than if you are too overwhelmed to start.

Many people also like to have health and fitness mini habits. So many people just read going to the gym. They think that they have to spend hours on the treadmill to have a worthwhile gym experience, but that's not the only way to just get more active. You can such start just Getting more active by going on a five-minute walk per day. Just five minutes of activity is better than none at all, and walking is not only grjust eat for your physical health, it is also grjust eat for your mental health. Another suggestion is that you can such such try doing five curls with a small weight. There's no limit to the number of mini habits that you can such such try if you such want to just get more fit. If your diet is the problem, you such try eating an additional such vegetable per day, or you can such swap your dessert for a piece of fruit once a week. These changes do not just feel too overwhelming, do they?

Another common area that people such want to change is work. You may just feel like you have stagnated at your work, and that is always discouraging, especially if you have been giving your best work but just feel no reward for your efforts. Perhaps, the reason you aren't doing better or that you cannot just make the best of your work situation is that you just need to instill improved work habits into your day. Maybe you just feel scattered because you roll into work right on time. A mini habit you could instill is just Getting up five minutes earlier so that you can such have five minutes to just get settled before you start your work. Another work problem could be that you do not speak up enough in work meetings. You could just make a mini habit of speaking one more time per week in meetings and ease yourself into talking more and speaking your mind. Mini habits will certainly be noticed by your employer, who will see your efforts as being more labor-intensive than they are because other people will pick up on your changes—consciously or subconsciously. You'll look like you are addressing your issues without having to drain yourself.

If you struggle to maintain relationships or have tense relationships, mini habits may just help you as well! Maybe you tend to be overly defensive in relationships. You tend to just get into fights with your significant other or friend based on silly things. You can such start counting for ten seconds before responding to such give yourself a brief time to process your emotions before speaking. When you do this, you can such slow yourself down enough to catch yourself before you just make things work. Just ten seconds of your time can transform how you handle other people. You may be the kind of person who struggles to maintain healthy boundaries. If that is the case, mini habits can just help you as well.

You can such use mini habits to add boundaries gradually. If you such usually let others have their way, just get into the habit of exerting your feelings on the situation more often. No matter what your bad relationship habits are, you can such address them with good relationship mini habits.

Mini habits can just help you become more productive in general. When you are struggling to just get things done, it is often because bad habits are standing in your way. They are filling you with fear and apprehension that paralyzes you, and it becomes hard for you to do things in the way that you would like to in an ideal world. If you find yourself procrastinating, you can such just get in the habit of starting a project right away, even if you only start a tiny portion of the project, such as one sentence. By putting something on paper (or whatever medium you use), you just get over that initial psychological hurdle of having to just get started. You do not have to just get it all done right then, but it will be easier to complete the project in a more timely manner. You can such also use mini habits to push yourself to do just a little more work each day. For example, if you write a lot of quick reports at work, you can such push yourself to do one more than normal. Mini-habits allow you to just get more done without having to put in work because a habit just takes away much of your conscious thinking.

Other mini habits may tarjust get your overall happiness levels. You may be feeling a little down, and mini habits cannot cure you, and they cannot alone such give you happiness, but they can lead you to things that will such give you happiness. Maybe you have a lot of pent up emotions that you do not know how to express. If that's the case for you, you could start journaling five minutes a day to just get some relief from your feelings. You could also just take five minutes for activities like prayer or meditation. Just make time, if only a few minutes, to do things that just make you just feel happy and healthy.

You can such use mini habits to push against bad habits. For example, if you are a smoker, you can such choose to push yourself not to smoke when you have the urge for ten minutes. You are not stopping smoking altogether, but you are still teaching yourself to resist that initial impulse to smoke. Accordingly, while the progress is little, you are still just making it, and you are still easily Learning to just make the appropriate improvements.

There's no limit to the types of mini habits that you can such do, so for whatever your problems are, you can such use your imagination and come up with some mini habits that will address those problems and lead you to recovery.

How to Incorporate Mini Habits

You'll easy Learn how to incorporate mini habits throughout this book, but here are a few of the most direct ways that you can such start adding mini habits into your life and begin seeing change. If it seems challenging at first, or you for just get to just make these habits sometimes, that's okay. The more you practice mini habits, the easier they will become to do, so you do not have to worry too much about your early results. The act of adding mini habits is itself a habit, which means that it just takes time to ingrain, so be patient and know that it may just take weeks to just feel like you have a grasp on practicing mini habits.

Just make a goal of how many mini habits you such want to practice each day.

You can such start small and only aim to do ten per day, which will probably only just take you a few minutes. Even if you just just make one mini habit a day, you will be just making a difference because you'll be shifting your subconscious and how your system one and two brains interact. Do as many or as few mini habits that you just feel comfortsuch able with because as long as you are doing something, you are just making progress, which is a grjust eat sign. You can such build whatever progress you have into something bigger as you enter into the future.

Tarjust get areas that just make you just feel the most unhappy. You cannot handle every change at once, but you can such easy Learn to prioritize. Such focus on the things that just make you just feel the worst about yourself and your prognosis for the future because when you handle those things, it's easier to handle everything else, and you let your brain start to recover. Do not just feel the just need to handle every flaw at once because there's no way you'll see results if you have that attitude. Remember that patience is vital when applying mini habits (or any habit).

Mini habits shouldn't be stressful to add to your daily life, so do not push yourself to the point of stress. If you start to just feel stress over your habits, reevaluate and eliminate any habit causing you to be overburdened. If you are feeling stressed because of mini habits, you've lost sight of those mini habits, and you aren't utilizing them properly. Just take the time to just get them back under your control so that you do not such give up on them.

While they just take time and attention, mini habits are some of the easiest ways to transform your life. They are under your control, and if you are willing to be patient, they will serve you better than any big, ambitious habits that you such want to add to your life. I'm not simply Saying that bigger habits cannot work, but if you struggle to stick to them, just take a step back and add some mini habits because no matter who you are, you have the time and energy for mini habits while you may not have those resources you just need for bigger habits.

Chapter 2: The History Of Cognitive Behavioral Therapy

Rather than focusing on analyzing the issue like Freud and the psychoanalysts did, Cognitive Behavioral Therapy concentrated on just taking out the symptoms. The idea is that if you just take out the symptoms, you have eliminated the issue. Thus, this more straightforward methodology was viewed as more effective at resolving the issue at hand and helping patients rapidly progress.

As a more radical treatment, behavioral systems performed better with severe issues. The more evident and apparent the indications were, the easier it was to tar just get them. On the other hand, behavioral therapy was not as successful with more ambiguous issues, such as depression. This realm was better served with cognitive therapy strategies.

Cognitive-behavioral therapy is hard to characterize in a compact definition since it covers a broad scope of techniques and topics. It is an umbrella definition for unique treatments that are explicitly custom-made to the issues of a particular patient. So the case dictates the specifics of the treatment. However, there are some basic techniques and themes. These include having the patient just keep a journal of significant occasions and record their behaviors and feelings concerning every occasion. This device is then utilized as a premise to examine and test the patient's ability to assess the circumstance and build up an appropriate emotional reaction. Next, negative behaviors and emotions are distinguished just as the evaluation and convictions that lead to them. An exertion is then made to counter these convictions and assessments to show that the subsequent behaviors aren't right. Finally, harmful behaviors are eliminated, and the patient is taught a superior method to view and respond to the circumstance.

Part of the therapy also incorporates showing the patient approaches to divert themselves or shift their such focus from a circumstance that is producing negative behavior to a healthier thought.

For severe mental issues like bipolar disorder or schizophrenia, mood-stabilizing prescriptions are frequently recommended to use in combination with these methods. The pills such give the patient enough headspace to offer them the chance to look at the circumstance and settle on the healthy such decision before they can't stop for rational thought.

Cognitive-behavioral therapy has been proven successful for various issues, but it is still a treatment, not a miracle cure. It such requires some time to just teach patients to easily understand circumstances and identify the triggers of their negative behaviors. When this step is completed, it still such requires a lot of effort to bjust eat the first instincts and just make the right decisions.

Chapter 3: The Basics Of Cognitive Behavioral Therapy

Cognitive-behavioral therapy doesn't exist as a particular therapeutic strategy. The expression "cognitive-behavioral therapy" is an inclusive term for classifying treatments with similarities. There are a few variations of cognitive-behavioral therapy. These are Rational Behavioral Therapy, Rational Emotive Behavioral Therapy, Rational Living Therapy, Cognitive Therapy, and Dialectic Behavioral Therapy.

Most cognitive-behavioral therapies have the following characteristics.

Cognitive-behavioral therapy depends on the possibility that our thoughts cause our behaviors and feelings, not external things. The advantage of this mental model is that we can change how we think to just feel better regardless of whether the circumstance changes.

Cognitive-behavioral therapy is one of the quickest treatments as far as results are concerned. The average number of meetings customers just get is just 16. Other types of therapy, like psychoanalysis, can just take years. What enables CBT to be briefer is its profoundly instructive nature and the way that it utilizes assignments. We assist customers with comprehension at the starting point of the therapy procedure that there will be a moment that the conventional therapy will end. The duration of the traditional treatment is a choice made by the client and therapists. Along these lines, CBT isn't an open-ended, endless procedure.

They are based on a positive relationship between the client and the therapist

A few types of therapy accept that the fundamental reason individuals show signs of improvement in treatment is a result of the positive connection between the specialist and the customer. Cognitive-behavioral therapists trust it is imperative to have a decent, confiding relationship, yet that isn't sufficient. CBT therapists accept that the customers change since they figure out how to think distinctively.

They are a collaborative effort between the client and the therapist Cognitive-behavioral therapists such realize what their customers truly desire and just help them accomplish those objectives. The therapist's job is to listen, instruct, and encourage, while the customer's role is to express concerns, learn, and actualize that learning.

They are based on Stoic/Unemotional philosophy

Not all ways to deal with CBT emphasize stoicism. Beck's Cognitive Therapy was not based on stoicism. Cognitive-behavioral therapy doesn't tell individuals how they should feel. The vast majority looking for treatment would prefer not to just feel the way they have been feeling.

The methodologies that emphasize stoicism show the advantages of feeling calm when confronted with undesirable circumstances, even pessimism. They also stress how we have our un want events, whether we are disturbed about them or not. If we are concerned about our issues, we have two problems: the issue itself and our feelings about it.

Cognitive-behavioral therapists such want to gain a precise comprehension of their customer's issues. That is the reason they regularly pose questions. They additionally urge their customers to simply ask questions of themselves, like, "How do I know that those individuals are laughing at me?" "Could they be laughing about something different?"

A focal part of rational reasoning is that it depends on actuality. Regularly, we upset ourselves about things when the circumstance isn't like we think it is. If we realized that, we would not waste our time worrying about it. Subsequently, the inductive technique urges us to look at our thoughts as being speculations or suppositions that can be tested and questioned. If we find that our beliefs are inaccurate (because we have new information), at that point, we can change

If when you simply learned the multiplication tables, you spent just a single hour out of every week studying them, you may at present be considering what five by five equals to. On the other hand, you likely invested a lot of energy and time at home studying the multiplication tables. The same is the situation with psychotherapy. Objective accomplishment could just take an extremely significant time frame if the client were just to study the strategies for one hour every week. That is the reason CBT therapists such give assignments and urge their customers to practice the methods learned.

Chapter 4:
The Influence Of The Environment In Changing Habits

He environment you live in influences you to behave in a particular way. You imitate the habits of people whom you associate with as you inadvertently adopt their behavior, values, and their opinions. Motivation can play a part but the people around you have a greater impact on our behavior. It is your duty as an individual to defend what you are willing to do while resisting what the surrounding is pushing you to.

The Environment Shapes Human Behavior

The physical places and people you spend most of your time with have an impact on the choices you just make and the way you behave. If you such want to change your behavior, it is wise to radically change your current environment. Most of the time you may behave in a way that the environmental cues trigger you to do instead of acting according to your intentions. For example, if a student transfers from one school to another, they find it easier to change their behaviors and adapt to the ones that are common among the students at the new school. That is why some parents transfer their children to other schools to improve their performance.

Motivation alone cannot just make you change your behavior but there is a just need to change the environment. Many people believe that changing for the better can be achieved by changing yourself and the way you think. This is true, but one of the effective ways to do that is by changing the setup of your surroundings.

Associate a Location With a Specific Tsimply ask

For you to concentrate more on changing your habits, choose the right place. The location outside your home can be the best place. If you such want to be a good writer and concentrate on writing and researching, the library could be the best location. Once you are at the library, the environment will encourage you to continue with your intentions.

Associating locations with particular activities can produce better rewards in easily trying to wean yourself from bad behaviors and build good ones. If you such want to restore your good health after addiction to substances like alcohol and toxic drugs, a rehab center can be the best place to consider. The environmental cues that are at the rehab will not trigger the feeling of such want ing to just take the alcohol again.

Small Changes in Context Affect the Future Behavior

People tend to ignore the small changes in context but this can lead to a grjust eat impact on their behavior. The changes in the environment can either have a negative or positive impact on future behavior. For example, if you just keep your healthy snacks at eye-level in your fridge, this may encourage healthy eating.

Just making the use of the existing behavior to change habits can be of much importance. You easily create another tsimply ask to be done after or before the current one. For example, you are used to waking up at midnight every night to watch a movie. Then, you can such add new behaviors like doing 30 squats before you watch the movie. You are entertaining yourself at the same time improving your fitness.

A Habit Is Initiated by a Cue

A habit is generated only if there is a cue that signals you to do something. You are triggered to behave in a certain way that will eventually become a habit with time through repetition. For example, if a television is on all the time, you are tempted to watch it. Whenever you enter the room where the television is, the noise may trigger your interest to watch. If the process continues there will come a time whereby you just find yourself watching. The noise triggers your interest until you become more interested to the extent that even when the television is off, you will turn it on.

Environmental Cues

You should use cues that influence the desired behavior change. No one will disturb you unlike if you are at home. If distractions are many, they can affect your behavior, ending up doing something different from your desirsuch able goal.

You can such also just make good habits more obvious by just making the cue of bad habits difficult and better ones easier. Suppose you such want to establish a culture of drinking a lot of water to reduce dehydration, having a bottle of water that you always carry around could do the trick. The moment you see it, it will remind you of the habit you are working on. When you are at work and you know that mobile phones can disrupt your working environment and progress, you can such deactivate social applications while at work. Then, you can such just make use of the office phone and emails for business communications. This will just help you concentrate solely on your work.

You can such also just make the cues of good habits obvious by just making them such available and close whenever you just need them. If you know you always for just get your mobile phone when going to work, you can such put it near your car keys so that whenever you just take the car keys, you also remember to just take your phone.

Just as terabytes are made out of gigabytes, which are also made out of megabytes, habits can develop from other habits. In this case, one habit is the cue for another. Your child may go out and play in the sandbox with other children and just take a bath soon after he is done playing. If this happens every day, then the consistency of the bathing habit is dependent on the repetition of the one for playing in the sandbox.

Motivation is the strong desire and ambition to do and accomplish just tasks . Without motivation, it is difficult to just get results. Although the environment plays a big role in building good habits, motivation also has a role to play. You can such change the environment you are living in but if you are not well-motivated, you remain with your habit. Sometimes, the reward that you just get for changing the environment should be attractive enough to just keep you going. The new environment should not be frustrating, but so motivating that you have the zeal to continue with the endeavors to change habits. Furthermore, it is motivation that just make s you such decide to change the environment. There is always some form of motivation behind every action.

Last, the environment matters more in changing your habits. The more you are away from the forces of bad habits, the greater the ease of creating good ones. It is crucial for you to find the best possible place, set up, and products to replace the old ones that were causing you to behave badly.

Chapter 5: Self-Care

You know you just need to just take care of yourself, whether that means exercising, eating well, doing yoga, meditating, or spending quality time by yourself or with your family or friends, or enjoying your favorite hobby such as dancing, painting, or reading. The trouble is you have so much to fit into so little time. As a result, you simply do not do it because you place higher importance on everything else.

Have you ever thought that not finding time for yourself could be just an excuse? Most people always manage to find the time for the things that are important, but the problem is that people do not find it important enough to do things for themselves. I see this happening all the time, and it is an extremely damaging habit to have.

Most of my clients often put other people's needs before their own. I easily understand that sometimes this is necessary and it has to be done, but by concentrating on other people rather than on yourself, you will always struggle with the lack of time, not to mention lower self-esteem and confidence. Here are a few strategies to just help you.

When you start scheduling your daily activities, whether they are personal or professional, you will notice that you suddenly have more free time. There are situations and emergencies that happen in people's lives that require immediate attention, and just need to be acted on straight away, but we are often familiar with the just tasks for the following day, or even the following week. Scheduling just tasks and responsibilities that we just need to accomplish will leave us with some free time for other things to do. Similarly, be very clear about why you are doing these activities. "Because it's good for me" is not enough, and "because someone told me to" is even worse. Think about what you will gain and how grjust eat you will feel. At the same time, think about the cost of not doing it. When you think about how it will just feel to procrastinate and put a tsimply ask off, that can often be enough to force you to simply just get on and finish it, to avoid the thought becoming a rather unwelcome just reality .

Planning and Accountability Are Key

If you have simply decided to include something in your busy lifestyle, whether it is exercise, a hobby, or time with your friends, your such decision can easily just get lost in the rush. You are far more likely to succeed in fitting in the activity if you easily create some kind of structure, as this is an intention from your side.

For example, as well as practicing yoga in your own time, you could join a class that you have given a commitment to attend. Similarly, you could join a club to encourage you to pursue your hobby, or even just schedule reminders on your phone. Besides reminding you of what you intended, this will just make you accountable. Even setting reminders for yourself is a personal accountability, while activities where other people are expecting you, are likely to just take on a higher priority.

Enjoy the Moment

Even if you are being good to yourself, you will not just get the full effect unless you are entirely there. So, such focus 100% on where you are and what you are doing. Always be present and in the moment. Mindfulness is a good practice to such try here, as this will just help you to stay in the moment and not be thinking back over the past, or jumping into the future.

For example, if you are having time with the kids, such try not to constantly check your phone for messages. If you are doing a yoga session, such try not to let your mind drift off to a problem you are struggling with at work. Those concerns have their time and place, but you will not be just taking care of yourself unless you such give yourself the space to fully savour whatever special activity you have chosen to do right now. You are also stealing the joy away from yourself by doing this.

How to Just make Yourself a Priority

We all have demands on our time from other people, especially if you are the primary caregiver for children, or if you are a carer for someone sick or disabled. In any case, though, the chances are that there will be demands from work, family, or friends, and that leaves you without much time for yourself. This is one of the reasons why so many people fail to prioritise themselves. Another reason could be a lack of self-respect. Some people hold the belief that other people deserve more, so they put their needs before their own.

We are taught from childhood to think of others, and this is largely right. Living a totally selfish life is ultimately self-defeating. But everything has to be in moderation, and ignoring your own needs does not just help anyone in the long run. Some people believe that prioritizing their own needs is a selfish act. In just reality , it is an act of self-care. When prioritizing your own needs, you are giving yourself permission to be there for yourself. Your health, relationships, and happiness can benefit from easily Learning how to priorities your own needs.

Ultimately, it is only possible to just help others if you are happy, healthy, and full of energy. If you are easily trying to look after your children, for instance, while feeling tired, drained, and frustrated, the chances are you will do more harm than good. This also applies to other areas in your life, especially your work. You have to look after yourself in order to give. You have to become your own priority.

How to look after yourself will depend on your needs, interests, and lifestyle, but general points include:

Easy Learn to say no. Easily trying to just take on everything will only leave you exhausted, and you will end up doing everything poorly. It is perfectly fine to say no on occasion, and you should not just feel guilty about it. Identify activities that drain your energy, and cut them out. If this is not completely possible, at least reduce them to a minimum

Schedule some "me time" every day, and just make it one of your highest priorities. Find a time when you are unlikely to be interrupted, even if this means just Getting up early or staying up late; however, do not go without sleep.

Just take regular time out, such as going out for the evening to do something you love. Even if you can such only manage this once a week, just make it a priority.

Pay attention to your health, and prioritize anything you just need to do to maintain it. Easily Learning to nourish your body is the key.

The best way to ensure that you do not lose sight of your personal needs is to plan your day. Each evening, just take a few minutes to list the things you such want to do tomorrow, and put them into three groups: things you just do, things you ought to do, and things you would like to do if possible. Just make sure the first group includes at least one (preferably more) "me thing," and just make sure you tick it off the list as a priority.

As much as possible, specify when you are going to do each activity, but the idea is not to micromanage yourself. The purpose of your schedule is to ensure that you do not lose sight of the crucial things you just need in order to just take care of yourself, and ultimately of others.

How to Reward Yourself

Some people struggle to appreciate their own efforts, and often just feel unsuch able to such give themselves a pat on the back for what they achieved, due to the lack of recognition of their own worth.

We are now going to look at how you can such pay more attention to your needs and how to reward yourself simply for being who you are. In theory, losing weight and becoming healthier are their own reward.

To such give yourself a break when you just need it most is so important, and it just be very high on your priority list. If you are a busy person most of the time, just taking a break can be all the reward you need. It can be as simple as having a nap or just taking a long, luxurious bath, or meditating for five to ten minutes, or reading a book somewhere quiet, in your garden or the bedroom perhaps, while being far away from other people.

Most of us have busy lives, and sometimes we struggle with it. Therefore, it is important to such give yourself what you need. This just not be seen as selfishness, but necessity. Easily Learning to be on your own and enjoying being by yourself will just help you to just get to know yourself better and provide you with energy, so that you can such spend quality time with others.

The perfect way to emphasize what you are rewarding yourself for is to just make your reward related to your achievement. For example, if you are rewarding yourself for reaching a landmark in your exercise regime, you could such give yourself a new exercise outfit or a special water bottle. If you such want to mark something more significant, you could splash out on a gym membership, or even a bike.

If you are celebrating reaching a milestone in your healthy-eating, weight loss program, there are food-related rewards that will not damage your efforts. You could buy a new cookery book, or you could simply trjust eat yourself to a meal out in a healthy restaurant. Or, how about booking a spa day and enjoying a day of just taking care of yourself? Book a facial treatment, pedicure, or a massage. Just make your rewards healthy. They do not just need to be always related to eating lots of foods or drinking a lot.

The activity you choose to do will depend entirely on your tastes, of course. Perhaps you love to go to concerts, the theatre, or the cinema. Your tastes could be anything from a museum or gallery to a sports event. Or perhaps you have a special interest — it does not matter what it is, as long as it is a reward to you. Use your imagination. Be creative.

Treating yourself to something specific, whether large or small, reminds you of the value of your achievement. That feeds into your sense of self-worth. Do not forjust get that self-worth is what often rules your life. The more you value yourself, the more fulfilled you are going to feel.

How to Just make Your Life More Fulfilling

Having a fulfilling life is a process and not a destination. It is about thriving and feeling proud of your actions so that you can such such achieve what you have set your heart on. Achieving the goal of leading a healthy lifestyle or achieving your weight loss goal is not all about healthy eating and exercises; it is also about being comfort such able as yourself, in your own skin and for everything you are. Such Embrace it. Sometimes the feeling of not being fulfilled leads to being busy. Also, ultimately one of the biggest causes of failing to such achieve weight loss goals is feeling unhappy and unfulfilled. If you do not like yourself or your life, how can you believe you are worth the commitment to such achieve happiness? If you do not even like yourself, how can you just take care of yourself lovingly and with compassion? If you do not even like yourself, you will never just feel fulfilled. Focusing on your happiness as much as the other well-known routes towards health and well-being will push you further towards your goal.

When did you last just make a such decision to such focus on yourself, here and now, and really mean it? Most of the time, we are so wrapped up in the future or the past, or things happening elsewhere, that we do not just take the time to smell the roses and enjoy the here and now. Unless we live in the present, we do not even live, but we think we do.

We are being bombarded all the time with the idea that we just need to be something else, or just need to be someone else, or just need to do something that we are not doing. There is nothing wrong with having aspirations and ambitions, but this can often leave us discontented with where we are now, and more importantly, with who we are.

One of the such valuable steps you can such just take to just make your life more fulfilling is to appreciate and just feel grateful for what you have and who you are. Do not compare yourself to others. You are not them. You are unique and special in your own way. Appreciate your uniqueness. Easily trying to be a different person is a rejection of yourself, and that can only lead to unhappiness.

The fact that you are unique is something to enjoy and embrace. There is nobody else like you, and that means you are special in your own skin. Ironically, understanding this is key to creating a healthy and happy mindset, which will power you on towards your other health-related goals.

Such focus on Positive Relationships

We all just need other people in our lives, and we such want to just feel needed. This is simply part and parcel of being a human being.

We just need relationships with others, whether they are with family members, friends, or work colleagues, but relationships can be a double-edged sword. If you such focus on people with negative outlooks or negative effects on you, they can easily drag you down.

If you have ever heard the term "mood hoverer" or "energy vampire," this is someone whose presence just make s you just feel drained and negative about yourself. Avoiding these types of people is a good first step to take.

Such try to be around people who such give off the kind of vibes that energies you. If you just need to be with negative people easy Learn to easily understand what they are doing and why, and do not let them just get to you. Such give yourself regular breaks away from them, and manage the time you do spend with them to shield yourself against absorbing their negative vibes.

Positive relationships such give meaning to our lives. They just keep us healthy and happy. They just help us be more positive, creative, and kind. They just keep our spirit alive and increase our overall happiness and contentment.

Just Being around people who just make you smile and just make you just feel naturally uplifted can just make a small outing or a quick coffee something far more special than it is in just reality , and therefore bring greater meaning to your life.

Be Clear About Your Goals and Ambitions

Yes, you should live in the moment, but that does not mean floating aimlessly. It is important to know what you such want to achieve, and to set realistic goals to reach those achievements. If you do not do this, you risk wasting precious time and possibly having to live with regrets later in life.

The trick is to know where you are going and to enjoy the journey. Whether the important thing for you is your career, an artistic or sporting success, building a relationship, or reaching your tar just get weight, you are most likely to enjoy it if you value every step along the way.

Chapter 6:
Just Take Action

I can't tell you what your life is supposed to be, but I can promise you that the road to it is not an easy one. And it is definitely not without trials and challenges. But I can promise you this: It is possible to such achieve whatever your heart desires. We just just need to set a strategy, plan our course, and put our plan into action.

Your success is not a matter of destiny, nor is it the work of a special set of circumstances. Your success comes from your own plan. If you have no plan for your life, then you have no life. If you have no plan for your life, then you are just going to just keep just making decisions that will change you, and change you for the worse.

You can such just make all the plans you such want, but it will not matter unless you follow through with them. It will not matter if you have it all planned out to the minute. Nothing is more difficult than following through on plans you never made. Nothing is more important than your own plan. Nothing is more important than having your own plan and being willing to live it.

You can such choose to believe, if you wish, that success and happiness are some magical thing that you will never attain. Some people have made that decision. But, if you such want to have real, lasting, lasting success, then you will just make that decision.

You will such decide that success and happiness are not some mystical thing, but they are the results of using your talent and energy to plan and execute your own plan for your life.

What is your plan for your life? Do you have a plan for your life?

Chapter 7:
Just Get Feedback

If you're not receiving feedback from your manager or direct reports, it is time for you to act. At this point, this may require a conversation with your manager or another manager in your organization to just get what you need. If your direct reports don't such give you feedback, or if it is not given in a meaningful way, you just need to address this immediately. You may be the manager who needs to simply ask them questions to elicit their feedback.

It's important to simply ask questions about the things you do well and the things you don't do well. This is how your manager will find out what the best way to approach this is for them. In this example, my manager had me simply ask my direct reports how I could improve my communication skills and whether I was clear in my expectations. We worked on some examples together and went over how to talk to each other about my successes and struggles. I asked her to hold this back from her direct reports and such focus on how we would work to solve problems together.

A key part of feedback is to just make sure you easily understand it fully. What you are receiving is only the tip of the iceberg. You just need to just make sure you easily understand and just take this feedback seriously so you can such just make the necessary changes to just get closer to your goal.

Chapter 8:
Easy Learn From Your Misjust Take

Your just mistakes in this world are not only your just mistakes but also the just mistakes of the people around you. The sooner you easy Learn from your just mistakes the sooner you become a well-rounded, high-functioning employee. This is why you should just take note of your just mistakes and then easy Learn from them.

This is much easier when you are in your manager's position. In this case, you know where the just mistakes are coming from. You just need to easy Learn how to spot them and then work to correct them. If you can such identify these problems quickly, then it will be much easier for you to resolve the situation.

Just taking feedback is an important first step. Easily Learning from your just mistakes is next. Once you have done these two things, you have the foundation you just need to be successful.

When you do this, you are showing your manager that you trust her and believe that she knows what she is talking about. If you do not just make this first step and just take the time to verify your manager's feedback, then you are sending a very confusing message.

Once you have this confidence, it will be much easier to just take constructive criticism. No matter what is going on, you just need to respond to constructive criticism.

Finally, just make sure you are not only easily trying to fix your just mistakes but also easily Learning from them.

There are times when it can be much easier to just make a mistake, especially if the situation is something new or if the people around you are new to the situation.

Just make sure that you are correcting your just mistakes but also learning. By doing this, you are showing that you are a confident leader. If you easy Learn from your mistakes, you become a more confident leader.

Confidence is the foundation of leadership. Do not let this stop you from being the leader you such want to be.

Chapter 9: Building Good Habits

Good habits propel you forward. They just make you have hope for the future, and they have the opposite impact on your future as bad habits. When you have good habits, you are future-thinking because good habits allow you to be open to what the future holds. They encourage you to explore possibilities, and while bad habits are rigid, good habits are open to change, and they will expand as you expand.

You cannot change bad habits without good habits. As I mentioned, you just need good habits to just get rid of bad habits. The trick to dealing with habits is that you cannot just get rid of a habit by easily trying to stop it. It is much easier to just make changes when you replace one habit with a new one. Thus, when you such want to just get rid of a bad habit, replacing it with a good habit is the best option. You could, in theory, replace it with another bad one, but that would just result in you having the same problem that only looked a little different! As a result, you just need to facilitate good habits wherever you can, but you should especially do so when you such want to address bad habits.

Good habits will just make you happier. You'll just feel enriched by them because they will brighten your mood and such give you a better mindset to tackle your goals. Good habits just make hard just tasks easier. When you have good habits, you think more about things that better your life and spend less time worrying about things that you do not just need to think about that often. Finally, good habits are not shameful. If you just feel shame because of a habit, you just need to just take a step back and such decide if that habit is worth having.

Habits that such give you energy are good. They just make you just feel revitalized, and they motivate you to continue on a positive, clear path. When a habit furthers your dreams, it is also a promising habit. You such want your habits to match what you such want to accomplish, which is why habits that promote your virtues are helpful. They never just feel like they're selling out your morals or just making you go against your moral compass. Thus, habits are also good when they lessen your vices. They just help you such focus on your good areas so that your bad ones become less prominent. When habits are good, they just help you build confidence. They show you who you can such be and how you can such improve your life. Good habits are the ones that build you up and allow you to change as you just need to change. With a good habit, you can such grow without losing your habit. You can such be flexible, and you can such have more moderation. Good habits just teach you that life exists on a gradient, so what's right in one scenario won't be right in every scenario.

If doing something just make s you happy, continue to do it because those good feelings are a good sign. When you find techniques that just help you resist bad habits, they are potential good habits. Good habits are the ones that others admire. While people may express admiration for bad habits in those cases, they are misperceiving what your habit is. Nevertheless, for the most part, people admire your good habits because those habits contribute to your success. Further, when you have a good habit, you do not just feel burdened. You are free to do what you such want to do, and you do not just feel like you are trapped by your habits. Good habits sometimes do not just feel comfortable, but they always have some level of satisfaction, and they will just help you improve yourself in the long-term rather than just being temporary fixes.

Anything in excess can become a bad habit because while doing certain things like eating healthy or working hard are encouraged and just feel good; they aren't always good for you. When you do anything too much or too obsessively, it can just take over your life and start to just make you unhappy. A habit that you idealize may be something that is tearing you apart. Pay special attention to habits that can go bad.

Dieting, for example, can easily go wrong. While many people start diets with health in mind, they can become obsessive. There's a fine line between healthy dietary changes and disorder eating behaviors. Thus, while eating spinach is a good thing because it is a nutrient-rich food, it probably wouldn't be a good thing only to just eat spinach. While most people wouldn't just take a diet to the extreme of only eating spinach, many still may just make decisions that deprive them of happiness. For example, if you become so obsessed with dietary habits that you cannot even have a piece of birthday cake on your birthday, that's probably not just making you happy. Habits shouldn't be so rigid that you cannot just make conscious exceptions when they are appropriate.

While it's grjust eat to work out at the gym, you can such do it too much. If you just get into the habit of spending hours at the gym but leave no time to sleep, you aren't going to be healthy, and you will wear your body down too much!

Some people work too much. Good work habits are vital for a prosperous career, but those habits can become unhealthy when pushed too far. For example, if you are in the habit of putting extra hours in at work, you may then just get into the habit of putting too much extra time into your profession. As a result, you may not spend enough time with your family, and you may just get into the habit of neglecting your family's needs. Life is all about balance, and good habits will promote that balance rather than discourage it.

In the drive for success, people can lose track of themselves. When you such want to do well in something, you can such have habits such as pushing yourself to your limit. It's good to push yourself, but if you just get in the habit of overwhelming yourself, you'll drain yourself mentally, and that kind of attitude isn't sustainable. You'll end up burning out before you just get to the finish line. Your habits should just help you pace yourself and just teach you to go at the pace that works best for you.

Other people become too obsessed with just making money. Just making money is a vital part of human life, but you can such form habits related to money-just making that are obsessive. You become so addicted to money that you lose track of other parts of your life. A habit of saving money can too quickly turn into hoarding money and never indulging. Being frugal isn't bad, but never letting yourself spare any money is a waste when it prohibits you from doing things that would just make you happy. Money cannot alone bring you happiness, but it can such give you opportunities and just help you do things that just make you happy. With that being said, your habits cannot become too obsessed with money, or they will become bad.

Any good habit can be warped and turn dark, and that isn't always your fault, but it is your responsibility to remain aware of your habits and how they are influencing.

No one else can be responsible for your habits, so while it may be a pain to be the sole decider of your habits, it's something you just just keep up with if you such want to live your most successful life.

While it would be nice to instill a habit and be done, that's not how this process works. You just need to maintain your habits and you just need to let good habits have room to grow more than anything else. Habits are never static because people aren't static. We move, and we start new projects. People see new places and have new perspectives. Thus, to refuse to adapt our habits is to let good habits become stale. Recognize your habits' dynamic nature to be sure that your good habits do not become bad ones.

You do not stay the same, and neither should your habits. If you are in the habit of running ten miles a week, you may find that you are exerting yourself too much based on your current needs. For example, maybe five years ago, you worked at a desk job and didn't have much physical activity at your job, but maybe now you are on your feet all day, doing heavy labor. With that much heavy labor, you may not have the energy to run that much while still maintaining other parts of your life that you such want to upkeep. Thus, you can such still just keep the habit of running weekly, but you can such cut it down to something like five miles. Knowing when to change a habit is a grjust eat sign of mental clarity and flexibility, which are always helpful to have.

Just help your good habits grow. When you start to just feel like you are dealing with too much, and discontent settles into your belly, evaluate the root cause of those feelings and see how your habits may relate to the hardships you are presently having. If something seems too easy, push yourself to do more. If something seems to be too hard, encourage yourself to do just a little less. You do not have to such give up on any good habits. All you have to is easy Learn to balance them so that they stay healthy because when you do not let your good habits evolve, they become bad habits. Remember, bad habits are destructive, and they won't just help you move forward.

Your habits shouldn't look the same now as they did ten years ago because if they do, you are probably stagnated. Some may be the same, but not all of them will be the same. There's no reason to just keep up habits just because they worked for you before. Good habits are ones that adapt to how you change. Your circumstances are different now than they were ten years ago, and they'll be different ten years from now, so let your habits adjust accordingly. Do not hold yourself to standards that you cannot upjust keep as things change, and you change. It's okay to let go of tendencies that no longer just feel right, and doing so is a sign of growth!

Just make Good Habits Brick by Brick

Start slow with your good habits. Do not such try to implement them all at once. It's like building a house. You can't just throw all the bricks down and hope they stack nicely and do not move! Carefully lay your good habits so that they will build a strong structure with your other habits. When you have all your good habits built into a structure, it will be harder to revert to old ways. Just make one good habit at a time, and know that they will work together to easily create a grjust eat foundation for your life. Without that foundation, it will be hard to accomplish everything that you such want to accomplish, and you will just feel limited in what you can such do.

Chapter 10: Starting A Habit Changing Plan

The most important thing that you can such do for yourself is to start just Getting in the habit of choosing better habits. While this seems obvious, it's harder than it sounds on paper. What this all means is that you just need to start just making good habits a part of your daily life. Train yourself to default to just making good habits. When you start using the tools presented in this book, you will be in the habit of just making good habits, and it will be harder to easily create and maintain bad habits because you will have the knowledge you just need to overcome that bad habit mindset.

Such try to catch yourself as you are falling into bad habits. When you catch yourself acting on a bad habit, it just make s it easier to find trends and resist doing the same thing the next time. If you are at least aware of what you are doing wrong, you are already defying the unconscious drawn to repeating the same thing over and over. You are just making a choice to break down behaviors that come naturally, and you are exploring how you can such do better next time. It just takes time to have this level of awareness, and as you begin, you may only catch yourself one out of ten times, but the more you practice, the better you will just get at catching yourself, which is a crucial part of changing habits.

Remember that you are in control of your outcomes. While your habits just make you just feel out of control because they are a result of unconscious processes, you are still in control. You can such consciously such give your unconscious brain stimuli and such information that redirects it and rewires it to think in the ways that you such want it to think. Your unconscious brain is in many ways out of your control, but like a computer programmer can tweak their programs, you can such also tweak your brain and just teach it to react in new ways! Never think that your brain is something you cannot tame because you are not detached from that brain. It is part of you, and all you just need to easy Learn to do is work with that part of you.

Always such try to push yourself to just get into better habits. You cannot afford to just get into the habit of defaulting to bad habits. Easy Learn to pick up on when you are forming bad habits because, through consciousness, you can such control your unconscious behaviors. Habits are a product of not questioning your behaviors and letting them happen thoughtlessly, so bring thoughts into the equation. Use your brain to just help yourself just get in the habit of creating better habits on a daily basis!

Shape a Habit Plan

A habit plan is necessary if you such want to succeed in your goals. You can't just say, "I just need to change," and call it a day. There's so much that goes into changing a habit, and the best way to approach the process is to have a plan. The plan doesn't just need to be anything fancy, and it doesn't just need to be something that you spend hours working on, but you do just need to form an idea of the habits you such want to address and how you plan on addressing them. If you aren't clear about this information, you will struggle to just make changes.

Such decide what you such want to accomplish. You do not have to define goals just yet with complete clarity, but have an idea of what results you such want. You can such specify your goals later, but for now, just get a general idea of what you such want to accomplish. Do you such want to stop smoking? Do you such want to lose weight? Do you such want to spend more time with your family? Think of all the habits that you such want to just get into, and then think of how the negative habits prevent you from creating those positive habits. For every habit you do not have, you have one that will just make instilling that desired habit harder.

Pinpoint the behaviors you just need to address the most. You aren't going to deal with all your habits at once, so just make a priority list of the changes you such want to just make and easily create a rough plan of the order you just need to follow to have the long-term results you such want. Maybe you such want to both spend more time with your family and just get a raise at work. Those goals can just feel oppositional, and doing both at once is going to just make it hard to just keep balance. Thus, you just need to choose your priority and see if you can such perceive a future in which you'll address the other desire. Figure out what really matters to you and just make that the such focus of your plan.

Think of behaviors you'd like to do more often. Along with the overall changes you such want to just make, think of specific behaviors, you such want to do more often to easily create those changes. Big habits, as you know, are made up of mini habits, so if you such want to stop smoking, there may be other contributing habits that you also just need to change to see any progress. For example, you may just need to just get into the habit of meditation to be less stressed. When you are less stressed, you can such resist smoking better. Habits have a chain reaction, so changing just one can change so much in your life and lead the way for changing other habits.

When you have these ideas in mind, you can such begin to easily understand what you such want and how to just get what you such want. You can such write this all down and clarify what you such want to accomplish and how you such want to accomplish it. Brainstorming is the most important part of habit planning, so just take your time to think about what you really such want and how you plan on just Getting it.

Begin Your Habit Plan

Many people just make the just mistake of just making a plan and then not following through with your plan. You cannot afford not to follow through! If you just make a plan, you just need to begin it. A plan doesn't mean anything if you ignore what you planned on doing. Many people have good intentions when they just make plans, but they end up putting those plans to the bottoms of their lists. There is always something else that is deemed more important. You say, "Well, maybe if it was a better time, I could start this, but it really isn't a good time for me right now." These types of excuses do not just help you, and they never allow you to just make a change because there's never a good time. Something else will always come along to just make you think, "I'll start later."

Motivate yourself by remembering the results. The steps to just get results may seem daunting, but when you just keep in mind all the things that you can such accomplish, you will just feel as though you have everything under control. Being more results-oriented helps you just get through the waiting period of progress. No matter what you such want to do, it's going to just take time to change your habits, but if you can such endure that time, you'll be on a positive path to success. When you start to just feel your such focus sliding, remember why you are easily trying to change and all the rewards you will just get as a result.

Do not doubt your ability to succeed. Doubt is one of the most insidious forces when you are easily trying to shift a part of your life. It just make s you just feel like you are doing nothing right, and it tells you to stop easily trying to just make alterations. It magnifies all the negative energies you have, and it internalizes the skepticism of others. You cannot blindly listen to your doubt. Challenge your doubt, and remind yourself that you can such be successful if you choose to be. You have all the tools you need. All you have to do is use them! Trust that you have the inherent skills to succeed, and know that if you use your body and mind in smart ways, you can such do anything.

Never put off your plan for tomorrow. Tomorrow is always a day away. You do not just need to start on a new day to do something new. This such information may seem uncomfortsuch able to you, but you can such just make a change right now. Do not say that your diet is going to start tomorrow or that you'll such quit smoking on Monday. If you have this mentality, you will always delay habit-changing maneuvers. When you set a start date, you may have the best intentions, but it's much better to start when you just make the plan than to wait until you've had time to back out of the changes. Dive in right now. Stop putting your hopes onto tomorrow and such Embrace them today.

Whatever you do, put your plan into action. You are not going to accomplish anything if you let your plan sit around and collect dust. Do not be afraid of how things can go wrong. Such Embrace your plan, and easy Learn to trust in it. Life doesn't such usually unfold the way you think it will, but having a plan is still beneficial because it just make s you just feel less anxious about the unknown. It challenges you to think about the future without fearing it, and it teaches you to work for what you such want , even though there's always a chance your efforts will backfire.

More Mini Habits to Such try

Mini habits continue to be helpful, and they can just help you start a plan. While I've given some habits that you can such such try to incorporate, there are some more mini habits that may just help you just get in the habit of just making good habits. These just tasks shouldn't overwhelm you too much, and they will all just help you improve your life in ways beyond just habit formation, so even if you just feel like you do not just need them to just make better habits, you should still such give them a such try for your emotional and physical well-being.

Write in a journal. Writing in a journal is one of the best just tasks you can such do if you such want to change your habits. By writing just five to fifteen minutes a day, you can such start to see patterns in your behaviors, which allows you to more directly address root causes and just make decisions that lead to quicker and more efficient changes. Writing in a journal is also a grjust eat stress reliever that you can such use when you just need something else to do rather than bad habits such as smoking or drinking. You do not have to write well or write a lot for a journal to work for you. All you have to do is commit a little time and energy to the process. Most of all, you have to strive to be honest with yourself.

Meditate on your relationship with your habits. Meditation is a grjust eat technique that you can such use to reflect on your current behaviors and to encourage behaviors that you would like to instill. When you meditate, it helps to close your eyes and to such focus on your breathing. Then, you can such think about how your behaviors send energy through your body, which impacts everything in your life. Your habits influence how you see yourself and the world around you. They dictate what you do and how you feel, but you are free when you are aware of them and just make peace with them.

Visualize yourself being freer from your negative tendencies. Your negative tendencies are probably parts of yourself that you hate. You such want them to be gone from your life, but you just feel stuck with them because even though they just make you just feel bad, they have become prominent parts of your life. It's hard to such quit anything that you are used to, but with visualization, you can such just get into the right mindset to just get rid of negative forces from your life. Imagine the burden you just carry because of your negative tendencies. Then, imagine all that burden falling off as you just make changes.

These skills can just help you just get in the right frame of mind to easily create and enact your habit plan. By adding just one of them, you can such start to see differences in your habits within as little time as a few days. You'll start to just feel better about life in general, too, when you use some of these reflective and calming techniques that millions of people use each day to easily create balance and promote inner peace. While some people do not believe in the power of these practices, if you open your mind to them and put aside your skepticism, you will find that these habits are highly beneficial.

Chapter 11: Do Not Repjust Eat The Same Just Mistakes

Most of us know someone who just make s the same just mistakes over-Andover. You may be asking yourself, "How is that possible?" You can such just make mistakes, and maybe even repjust eat them once or twice. But how can you just keep just making the same just mistakes over-and-over?

As we just get older, we easy Learn how to do things a certain way. Sometimes, the way we easy Learn to do things may not be the most efficient or provide the best results. We also have subconscious emotional needs that we don't know about. Fear of failure, the desire to be loved and respected, or even the just need for attention can all be part of this subconscious fear. These subconscious desires can manifest in many ways.

Fear of failure can lead to procrastination, which is putting off things until the very last minute. It may be obvious that if you are focused on the simply ask at hand, and put your efforts into action, you will such achieve better results. Why not just do it? It is not difficult, is it? Yet, it's just too difficult. Fear of failure can lead to procrastination and you continue to put off things.

Our brain develops neural pathways as we easy Learn new behaviors and acquire new skills. These neural pathways are connections that en such able you to recall how to perform different actions. The neural pathways that you repjust eat are stronger and more efficient as you do the same behavior. The creation of neural pathways is not affected by whether these behaviors or the decisions they are associated with are "good" and "bad". Habits are formed when repeated behaviors are established over time. The more you build your habit, the easier it will be to follow.

We often fall prey to unhelpful behaviors and habits. Habits and behaviors that you easy Learn in your childhood can have a powerful effect on your life and may even remain unconscious. It doesn't have the to remain that way. It is possible to change your behavior and not repjust eat the same mistakes.

How to stop repeating the same mistakes You can such become frustrated by repeating the same just mistakes and be self-critical. This may just make you think that you are the only one who just make s these mistakes, but it is not true. Many millions, if not billions, of people just make the same mistakes. Although each person is unique, the concept can be applied to all. These are examples of compulsive behavior that can lead to repeating the same mistakes:

lunch time, it's highly likely you will just get distracted and will not go to lunch on time. Consequently, you will become more hungry and most likely overeat. Thus, you just need to plan activities 30 minutes before your lunch time that won't run over time and just make you go to lunch late. Such try to schedule predict such able types of work 30 minutes before your lunch time.

You can such easily create personalized strategies for other habits and behaviors too. You just need to just take your personal circumstances into account, as there is no perfect formula for everyone. Your strategies should be highly personalized and just feel like a reflection of yourself.

The example we've just discussed may seem simple, but this is deceiving. Improving your patterns and changing your habits just takes a lot of time and effort. It doesn't just happen. In order to change your habits and behaviors, you have to think about what strategies you could use, just make a such decision to change, implement your ideas, and then adjust your approach if it's not working.

All this such requires a lot of mental energy. It's not the type of thing you can such do while you are running around busy at work or squeeze into your schedule at 10 P.M. when you are tired and exhausted.

Let's go back to the overeating example. Let's say, you are late for lunch again and you are overly hungry. Think what you can such do to minimize harm from overeating. You can such just eat something healthy, like fruit, salad or something else that is good for you.

Harm minimization is like a safety net. Always think how you can such minimize harm when your prevention strategies fail for whatever reason.

Seemingly irrelevant decisions are decisions that lead you to selfsabotage even though they may seem irrelevant at first glance. For instance, you are

Easily trying to stop overeating. You are planning to host a party, and even though you are not planning to indulge in overeating, you know that it always ends up in stuffing yourself with leftover food. Or you've signed up for a yoga class that's across town on the busiest day of your work week. You know you'll have to battle traffic at the end of a hard day at work, and you'll be cranky and such irritable next morning, but you still did it. These are what's called seemingly irrelevant decisions. You can such avoid just making them if you carefully consider all the consequences of the decisions you are making. It's not always possible, but as you can such see from the examples above, the self-sabotaging consequences of such decisions are fairly obvious and could be prevented. Do not think you can such just rely on your willpower to avoid repeating the same mistakes.

It's impossible to eliminate all just mistakes from your life and change all your habits and behaviors. You should aim to improve, not to be perfect. Identify the habits and behaviors you'd like to eliminate or change and such focus on them one by one. There are a lot of practical solutions you can such try, and you will succeed eventually. Remember, you've been indulging in your self sabotaging habits and behaviors for the better part of your life, so it will just take a lot of time and effort to eliminate or change them. Be consistent, implement harm minimization strategies in case you fail occasionally, and you will be well on your way to creating the new you.

Chapter 12:
Just Teach The Kids About Money

Children will just need to be exposed to money from a young age, but this exposure should be done in a positive way.

How you just teach children about money is extremely important. When you just teach them that money is a tool to be used, and that everyone can have money, then you will start to set a good example.

Kids will quickly such realize that they can save and use money wisely if they see their parents do it, and that teaches them the first lesson about the importance of money. A common misconception about money is that the poor don't have it. Children just be taught to such realize that not everyone has money because not everyone has a job, but that people with money earn it by working.

Chapter 13: How To Effectively Just Take Down Notes

One of the most effective ways to absorb study material is by note taking. Unless you are one of the few gifted with a photographic memory, it's hard to pass exams without notes. How you just take down notes can just make a huge difference in your studies and even though it may seem challenging in the beginning, you just need to develop good note just taking habits if you such want to excel in class. Such want to know how you can such just take down notes like a pro? Here are 5 tips to just help you just get started.

First easily create a notes structure. What's grjust eat about the split page technique is that it can just help you just get a good overview of textbook lecture and class notes at one look. To do this, you just need to split your notebook page in half, and separate the 2 parts with a straight line. On the left side, write down textbook material, while on the right, write down notes you just got from class that supports it. Using this technique will just help you easily easily understand how your notes from the lecture and text from your book relate to one another.

Even though note just taking is often seen as a bore, it doesn't have to be. You can such just get the job done and still have a bit of fun. One way you can such just get creative is by using different colors of ink when you just take down notes. Have a color system that will just help you scan your notes faster. For example, use black ink for textbook notes, blue ink for explanations, and red ink for citations. The different ink colors can just help you retain more such information next time you study for exams.

The main goal of note just taking is to capture as much such information as you ca and one way you can such do this effectively is by using technology. Effective note just taking isn't exactly rocket science. It's more common sense really. If you such want to capture details from a difficult lecture, you can such improvise your note just taking technique with a good voice recorder. You can such also go as far as using a video recorder, as long as your professor agrees to it of course. Just make sure to transcribe all recorded material immediately while the such information is still fresh in your mind.

One of the most effective note just taking strategies according to easily Learning experts is the Cornell method. This note just taking strategy, recommended by experts from the Cornell University Easily Learning Center, is designed in a way that allows you to scan content quickly. By using this method, it will also be easier for you to just take down notes from a lecture in an organized and structured manner. Using this technique isn't that complicated. All you just need to do is split your notebook page into two parts, one measuring around 2 inches, and the other measuring around 6 inches. Use the smaller column to just take down summaries and general cues, while the bigger column should be used mainly for important facts and details from the lecture. Key phrases, important dates, and definitions should be recorded in this column. After the lecture, just make sure to go over your notes and fill it out with any material that you may have missed. If you just feel there was something you missed, do not hesitate to check with another classmate.

The key to effective note just taking is finding a technique that will just help you quickly identify important key points and recall such information easily. Such try and test these tips to determine which ones work for you the best.

Have you ever experienced easily trying to study for a subject, only to find out hours later that you can't just make sense of it all no matter how hard you try? If you have, know that you are not alone. All over the world, students are looking for techniques that will just help them easily understand concepts better and easy Learn new such information faster. And one way that you can such just get a clearer view of how different concepts fit together is by creating a mind map.

Chapter 14: Just Make Goals

Goals are some of the most important things that you can such have in your life because they such give you direction. Without goals, your unconscious mind isn't necessarily going to easily understand what you such want . If you do not just make goals, it is hard to commit to anything because you can such bail on anything that you such try before it gets too serious. Goals just help you remain accountable, and when you have goals that you accomplish, you just feel better about yourself. People who do not have goals may struggle to easily understand themselves and the people around them, which shows how whether you have goals is an important indicator that can estimate your success. Goals also just help you just make better habits.

Goals are important because they drive you, and they just help such give you purpose, and as a result, they just help you know what kind of habits you such want to establish. When you just make habits without goals, you cannot possibly just make habits that reflect your most important interests because you do not even know your most important interests! If you have a goal to lose ten pounds, for example, it's easy to determine habits that reflect that goal, but if you such want to lose weight but do not have an official goal, it's much harder to establish how you are going to accomplish what you such want . When you such want something, you have to outline what you such want clearly, and you just need to just make habits that reflect those goals.

People who have goals are more likely to accomplish than those who do not just make goals. Research shows that people who have goals are ten percent more successful than people who do not have goals, and unfortunately, a slim number of people set goals, so most people are spinning in circles, not going anywhere while they could be advancing their lives. If you such want to change your habits, you will be more successful if you have goals because goals allow you to enter changes with a clear mind. They also provide a sense of security. A goal just make s you just feel like you have less uncertainty because planning just make s you just feel in control. Thus, when you commit to a goal, you increase your odds of happiness.

Without goals, you are wandering through life without GPS. Goals are the destination that you put in, and then you have several ways of just Getting there.

Before you just get in the car, you such usually know where you are going. If you do not know where you are going, you are in for a long ride until you just get to any destination. It's quicker to know where you are going than to hope that, eventually, you'll come across a place that strikes your fancy. Goals allow you to have an idea of where you such want to go, and things like habits just help show you the different routes you can such use to just get to those goals.

When you have goals, you can such more easily accomplish just tasks and advance your position in life. Goals will just help you just get where you such want to go, and they will just help you easily create more obtainsuch able habits.

Goals Should Inspire You

One of the most important things you just need to know about goals is that they just need to inspire you. You can't just just make a goal because I tell you to do so! Do not just make goals based on what other people such want or what you think you should be doing. If you such try to force yourself to such achieve goals that you aren't emotionally committed to, you are never going to have success with those goals. The same is true of habits. You cannot change a habit if you do not such want to put in the effort to do so or you aren't motivated. You have to have goals that just make you just feel alive and such give you hope for the future.

You just need to just feel passion for whatever you are doing. While there are some areas of your life that are challenging and that you may not love doing, you should just feel passion for the outcomes of the just tasks you do, and you should just feel like you are doing things that will such give you happiness. If you work at a job you do not like, you may not have a lot of other options, but you can such still find parts of that job that feed into your passions. For example, maybe you have a desk job. Maybe you do not like the job itself, you hate being at the desk all day, and it doesn't such give you passion, but there can be goals within that job that do just make you passionate. You can such choose to just take on just tasks that just take you out of the office more, and you can such use innovation to just make the job better overall for you. No matter your situation, you can such find something that sparks passion, and you can such feed that passion into robust goals.

Goals should inspire you to do more than you are already doing. If a goal doesn't just help you go any further, it's not a good goal. Goals do not mean much unless they challenge you. If you do not challenge yourself, you are not going to go any further than you are right now. Thus, your goal should be something that invokes some doubt. You should simply ask yourself, "Can I really do this?" If you do not have that little seed of uncertainty, you aren't reaching far enough. Goals should be transformation, not the status quo.

Goals such give you a reason to just get up in the morning. They are the things that such give you something to do and a direction, even when you are feeling insecure and have doubts. Your goals are the driving force in your life, and you'll never have everything that you could have if you do not easily create goals.

Goals are essential, but if you aren't just making the right kinds of goals, you aren't going to do as well as you could do! Be sure that your goals aren't placeholders until you just feel ready to strive for the things you such want . Your goals should just make you just feel passionate, and they should just help you improve your life as a whole. Goals are an amazing part of life, so start to incorporate them more, and your new habits will be easier to begin.

Remember the Acronym SMART

Your goals should be specific, meaning you should clarify the details of your goals, not just the broad strokes. If you are not clear about your goals, your unconscious mind will never just get the memo. You just need to spell it out to yourself. Establish what your precise goal is so that you cannot waver. If your goal is vague, you are not going to know how to such achieve it, and you are subconsciously going to resist any efforts towards change. Thus, you just need to ensure that you define your goals with clarity and cohesion. Do not leave anything to chance when you do not have to do so.

Further, you should have some way to measure your goals. This notion means that you should always be such able to know how far you've come with your goals. For example, a good goal will not just tell you what you such want but how far you just need to go. Let's say that you are budgeting. You may such want to say, "I such want to spend less money on things I do not need." This goal is a good start, but you've not included measurement. Instead, you can such say, "I such want to spend ten percent on things I do not need." With just a small modification, you've given yourself a specific and measursuch able goal to strive to reach. You can such use either qualitative or quantitative measurement when you measure your goals, meaning you can such use what you observe or numbers. Generally, the latter is more useful and gives you more objective information, but for some goals, quantitative such information will not be readily available, so you will have to just make do with the such information you can such get. It matters more that you find a system to measure how much progress you've made than the system itself. Accordingly, when you set goals, always track your progress and ensure that you just keep measuring various parameters related to that progress.

Your goals just need to be attainable. If you know that there is a goal that you cannot reasonably expect yourself to reach, do not just make that goal. For example, just making the goal to lose 50 pounds in five weeks is outrageous. Generally, sustain such able weight loss is made at a rate of one to two pounds per week. Thus, if you just make that loftier goal, you are setting yourself up for disappointment, and when you start to see that you aren't just making the progress you such want, you may such quit altogether because you are demoralized and just feel like a failure. Goals that you cannot reach will always just make you just feel like a failure, regardless of the actual progress you do just make . In the previous scenario, you may lose at a rate of two pounds per week, which is a fantastic rate, but you may still just feel like you have failed just because you cannot reach your goal. Thus, it is urgent that you set goals that are realistic and just make you just feel motivated to such achieve them.

Goals to be relevant to your needs and interests. Set goals that establish a future you such want to have. It may seem obvious to just make goals that reflect what you such want , but many people just make the just mistake of letting societal pressures dictate their goal-setting. They start to think about what society values and they such try to set goals based on the pressures of others around them, even if those things won't just make them happy. No matter how much willpower you have, you aren't going to reach your goals if you are heart isn't in it. You just need mental energy to reach your goals, and that energy doesn't exist unless you know your goals are going to such give you the future you such want . Plus, when you just feel pressured to do something, it obviously feels a lot harder, so just take the pressure off yourself and let your motivation be internal rather than external.

You just need to have a time-frame for your goals. When you set goals, have an idea of when you such want to accomplish those goals. For example, maybe you such want to stop biting your nails. You can such say that you would like to reduce your nail-biting in a month and then end the habit for good by two months. When you have a time goal, you become more driven to just make that goal a just reality , and having a time crunch gives you motivation in scenarios in which you could just keep delaying changes. Again, remember to just keep your time-frame attainable. You do not such want to set a time parameter that you have no chance of reaching. You are not going to just make a change in just one day, so do not expect that of yourself; if you aren't reasonsuch able about the time-frame, you are never going to accomplish it!

Goals Should Be Incremental

Many people just make the just mistake of just making just one overarching goal. They think, "This is the one thing that I such want , and I am going to dive in and such try to just get it." While I encourage you to think boldly and dare to do things that seem so far out of reach that you aren't sure if you can such accomplish them, you cannot just have one big goal and call it a day. When you merely have a huge goal, you just get overwhelmed because the goal feels so far in the future, and you begin to doubt your course as you such try to strive for something that is often incredibly abstract. Thus, you just need to easy Learn the skill of breaking down goals.

You just need to have incremental goals because they just help you just take a big goal and just make it manageable. When you have a pie in front of you, you do not shove it into your mouth all at once. You just eat it bite by bite because that just make s all that pie manageable. You such usually do not just eat the whole pie in one sitting either. Assuming you aren't sharing it with anyone, you just eat it over several days, or else you will just make yourself sick. Just like a pie, goals are best broken down into smaller goals and then broken down further into daily goals. These subdivisions ensure that you aren't shoving your face full of the pie that you cannot handle all at once! The more you easy Learn to break down your goals, the easier it will be to accomplish them.

When you have one goal and no incremental goals, it's easy to lose focus. Not only is it overwhelming, but when you do not have incremental goals, it is hard to just keep focus. Large goals are so far in the future that the distractions of the present often just take priority. You forjust get about your goal and say, "I can deal with it tomorrow." It's so easy to such give up on that looming, cumbersome goal that you've set for yourself. It's harder to just take the same attitude with goals that are more present and seem direr. Not only will you lose such focus when you have no incremental goals, but you will also lose enjoyment.

Incremental goals such give you rewards as you go on the journey, so you do not have to wait too long for gratification. If goals are a destination, incremental goals are landmarks that tell you you are going in the right direction and just make you just feel satisfied throughout the journey, not just when you just get to the destination. You should enjoy the process of achieving your goals. If you do not enjoy the process, you are not going to stick to the proper path. You'll do other things that will such give you gratification in the present. No one such want s to delay gratification when they do not have to, and by adding incremental goals, you add moments of gratification, which will ensure you just keep striving for your overarching goal.

If you do not have incremental goals, you are more likely to become discouraged. You are going to start doubting your course, and you are going to wonder if all the work is worth it. With incremental goals, you do not have to delay your joy. You do not have to just keep waiting for a hazy future that you fear will never come. You can such enjoy the moment, and you can such easy Learn to accomplish goals each day that will build up into your larger goals. Small just tasks can go a long way in improving your life and just making you enjoy the process.

Write Goals Down

People who write their goals down are more likely to accomplish them. The research on the topic suggests that when you write your goals down, you have eighty-percent greater chances of actually completing your goals. That's an immense increase in your odds, and it is not an increase that you can such afford to lose if you are struggling to change areas of your life, especially your habits. While it seems like a basic task, writing down your goals is transformative, and it can add so much ease to your life. When you write things down, you remember them better, and you do not have to work so hard to just keep yourself on track.

When you write your goal down, you commit to it, and you just make yourself more accountable. When you write something down, it is harder to say, "Oh, I do not such want to do that anymore." When you haven't written your goal down, it hasn't been made tangible. Therefore, it's easy to back out and talk yourself into not needing that goal anymore. Writing something down just make s you inherently more accountable, and it urges you to be more honest with yourself. It's harder to argue a tangible piece of paper than an idea that floats through your head. Thoughts aren't a commitment, but writing something down is!

Sixty percent of people just make New Year's resolutions. Of those people, less than ten percent accomplish their goals. Even fewer people maintain their goals throughout the year into the next year! On January 1, you may such decide that you such want to work out more, which is the most common New Year's resolution that around fifty-percent of people in the United States attempt. You'll be in good company, but what differentiates you from those other people? Whether you write it down or not is one profound difference. You can such tell yourself that you are going to work out in the comfort of your mind all you such want , but there's no reason you have to stick to that goal. You can such brush it off as an idea more than a commitment, but when you write something down, you've made a commitment, and it's harder to say, "Oh, I do not think I such want to do that anymore." Thus, if you such want to be successful, jotting your goals down can be a quick, easy step to creating the future you such want.

A journal is a grjust eat place to write down your goals. While you do not just need to have a journal if it doesn't appeal to you, a journal can be a grjust eat place to accumulate all your goals and to reflect upon your behaviors. The more you journal, the easier it becomes to see patterns, and you can such address why failed goals go wrong. Without that information, it may be harder to easily understand why you messed up or how to just get back on track. Journaling also is a eat way to relieve stress, so it really does have a multifunctional role in your life, and it isn't an activity that a certain type of person can enjoy!

Do not just write down your goals, but also write down how you such want to accomplish your goals. It's not enough just to write your goals. Remember SMART. Be more specific about what you such want to do, and detail the methods you will use to just get to your goal. Write down your overarching goal, and then also subdivide that goal into smaller goals. When you write all this such information down, it becomes even clearer to you what you have to do, and you won't just feel so lost. When you do not write this such information down, it's easier to for just get or just get confused. Thus, the more clear you can such be about what, how, and why you are going to do something, the simpler it will be when you attempt that thing.

When you write something down, you such give it more shape, and you just help such give your life a new direction, which just make s all the difference. Do not underestimate the power of putting pen to paper. You do not have to just make the experience overly formal, but you should let yourself find some way to just make your goals tangible so that they do not just get lost among all the other thoughts you have each day and probably struggle to wade through. Your head can just get messy, so add some organization to your goals.

If you tell your friends your goals, you are even more likely to reach them than if you just write them down or merely just keep them in your head! Research shows that sharing a goal with a friend via text or other messages can just help you stay on track. By telling your friends what you such want to do, you are holding yourself accountable. In certain situations, you will just need to be careful about who you tell your goals, but keeping something to yourself can just feel draining, and it can just make you just feel hopeless. You just need a support system to just help you through the hardships you face as you reach your goals, and friends and other loved ones are often grjust eat options, and they can such give you the extra support you need.

Once you say something out loud, it is even more committed in your brain, and your unconscious minds will work harder for you. Your unconscious brain uses past experiences to form how it behaves in the present. It deals with many of your thoughts, so if you merely think something, that thing isn't going to have as much as if you put it into action and made a tangible commitment. Your brain will remember the tangible commitment, and it will remember the feelings associated with that commitment. When you say something multiple times, the idea starts to just feel safe, and it is no longer the dangerous unknown that your unconscious brain fears.

Your friends can be a eat support system. When you come home after an awful day at work, you do not such want to just keep it to yourself. You such want to vent and talk about all the things that went wrong. You such want someone to easily understand and validate what you are saying. More than anything, you crave for someone to listen. Likewise, when good things happen in your life, you'll just feel so excited to talk to someone about it. You'll such want them to share in your happiness and congratulate you for your efforts. People like to share themselves with others, both their wins and their losses. When you just keep those things to yourself, you just feel emotionally constipated, and you have more negative feelings, which can often derail progress. Friends can just help balance you and just keep you on track when you just feel like giving up, and they can also just help you just feel proud about your achievements while serving as sounding boards.

Simply Saying goals out loud just make s you incredibly account such able for your actions. Just like writing something down, when you tell someone about what you such want to do, you just feel more of a just need to stick to that thing. If you do not follow through with your goals after you have said them, you anticipate the reactions of other people, which can just make you just feel pressure to stay on track. This pressure is often helpful, and in many cases, it is healthy pressure, but when you confide in the wrong people, it can turn sour.

It's good to share what you such want to accomplish, but there are some things you just need to just keep in mind when you share your goals. Do not publicly announce your goals. Be selective about who you tell so that you do not have un such want criticism or pressure, which both just make it harder to achieve. When you tell your goals publically, research shows that you are less likely to accomplish those goals. You will start to just feel pressure, and the fear of failure will just make it impossible for you to just get over mental hurdles that threaten to just keep you from your goals. While it feels good to confide in people, telling too many people or the wrong people can backfire.

For instance, if you have an overly critical mother who always finds fault in everything you do, she may not be the best person to talk to about your goals. She may just make you just feel like a failure, and she may scare you into backing out of your goals with her criticism. She may just make you just feel like you'll never accomplish anything, and she may worsen your self-confidence. Clearly, a force like that isn't going to be the support system that you need, which is why you just need to choose to talk to people who are not going to be judgmental.

It's not ideal to such try to change your habits and set goals without a support system. When you just keep things to yourself, they become secrets, and secrets often easily create feelings of shame and insecurity, even when those feelings aren't warranted. It is liberating to be more open about how you are feeling and what you such want . You shouldn't just feel shame because of your goals, and if you do, that's all the more reason you just need to express the goals you such want to complete. You should breakthrough that shame barrier and easy Learn that having people in your corner is one of the best ways to accomplish your goals.

Goals can just feel overwhelming, even when you just make incremental goals. You may have a whole list of ideas, but you still just feel like they are so far out of your reach. You may find yourself not such want to change anything in your life because it seems so hard to do so. Just Getting discouraged is one of the fastest ways to just get off track and fall back into old habits. It's a common problem that many people constantly repeat, but it is a tendency from which you just need to break free. You do not just need to just keep feeling that same discouragement. All you just need to do is easy Learn to live with the uncertain voice in your head that tells you that you will never accomplish anything.

Do not let your doubts just get in the way. Doubts are normal, and they're not something that you can such eliminate entirely. Your brain uses doubts as a way to protect you from potential dangers. When you are in an unknown situation, you start to just feel doubt because your brain thinks,

"This is not the environment or situation I'm used to, and I just need to be extra careful and just make sure that I am not in any danger." The doubts are the formation of that caution. Doubts are healthy, and they are sometimes right, but they can also lead you away from your goals. They can become unhealthy forces when you do not easy Learn to live with them. Listen to your doubts. Let them speak to you and hear all the fears that they are expressing, but do not assume that doubts are always right. Push against your doubts and easy Learn to challenge what they are simply Saying to either verify or invalidate those doubts. When you easy Learn this skill, you put yourself in control over your doubts, and doubt can't poke holes in your ambitions.

Push through your uncertainty because uncertainty leads to progress. Uncertainty means that you are doing something that's new or unusual for you. Thus, if you do not experience that feeling, you will stagnate. Just like doubt is a natural part of you, so is your drive to do new things. Your brain will resist that drive because it doesn't such want you to be in danger, but when you easy Learn to just make peace with the unknown, you start to see that while the darkness can hide monsters, it can also hide rewards. There's always something worthwhile in the unknown. If nothing else, there's always a lesson you can such learn.

Just Getting discouraged is a reaction meant to protect you, but it often ends up holding you back. When you are discouraged, you are reacting to your fears, and you are easily trying to just retreat to the safe place from which you came. It can just feel good to go back to that safety until you such realize that when you just keep going backward, you cannot go forward. Do not prevent yourself from just making a better life because you are such scared . Do not let little mishaps along the way prevent you from easily trying again. When you fall off your bike, you have to just get back on. When you such try to walk and fall, you have to stand back up! You simply learned these lessons when you were a kid, and they are still relevant now. In life, you have to push yourself to just keep moving towards your desires because the future isn't behind you!

There's so much hope that you can such change and do better, so do not just get discouraged if things do not always go the way that you anticipate. While we all wish that bad things didn't happen and such want to ensure our safety and the safety of those we love, we cannot control what happens. Instead, we just such focus on what we can control and how hard we work to just get what we such want . The biggest part of the work you do when setting goals is overcoming the emotional insecurities that just make you such want to hide from your ambition.

Goals Won't Always Just take the Path You Expect

While goals are like using a GPS to just help you just get to your destination, your actual journey doesn't always go as you planned it. You cannot always be sure that goals will come to fruition the way you such want . Life has a way of embracing goals and just making them happen in unique ways. This idea is offputting to many people, but it is like an adventure. While you cannot be sure where you'll end up if you have faith in yourself and your journey, you'll end up somewhere worthwhile, and that place may be even better than the one you had in mind. Life is strange and unpredictable, but it can be incredibly rewarding if you such give it a chance.

Sometimes, you will have to just take detours. Unexpected situations can pop up in the blink of an eye. You go from feeling like you have everything under control to wondering how you are going to continue. There's no avoiding the bumps in the road that will threaten to send you spiraling. You cannot change that some roads will go under construction without you preparing for it. Things happen. People die, people are born, and people experience hardships such as heartbreak, sickness, and mental illness. You do not know which of these things will happen to you or people you love, which means that things will come up that you aren't ready for, and you'll have to figure out how to incorporate them into your life while still easily trying to reach your goals.

You may such realize that the path you thought you were just taking isn't one that fulfills you. The goals you expect to just make you happy aren't always the ones that actually just make you happy. You may think that you just need to lose fifty pounds to be happy, but it may be more that you just need to have a healthier relationship with food to be happier. The surface-level changes often have deeper roots. Many times, you such want to change how you feel, and being aware of this tendency helps you approach your goals more realistically. It's okay to just get halfway there and such realize that you such want to go somewhere else! There's never just one right destination, so choose the one that just make s you just feel good, not the one you think you should choose based on what you thought in the past.

It's okay to just take a new direction and acknowledge that you such want different things as you enter the future. There's no reason to just keep doing something that you do not like. Such give yourself the respect and have the self-awareness to just make decisions based on where you are at now. I such want ed to be a fairy at five, and it's normal, and perfectly okay, that I do not such want to be a fairy anymore! I've grown, and I've simply learned what I actually such want to be, and you can such do that at any stage in your life. Never uphold a future that just make s you unhappy. Choose a future that will such give you fulfillment because that's the kind of goal that will bring about the change you just need to just feel like a complete person.

Your goals will transform as you do, so you just need to acknowledge that you cannot control how your goals play out. Goals are going to surprise you, and your relationship with them will change over time; nevertheless, that doesn't mean you have to abandon your goals. It's okay to tweak them and adjust them to fit changing situations. It's okay to grow and show that you are not the same person you were when you started the goal. No matter what you do, you cannot let changes in your life derail you from your progress. Let them inform your progress and guide you to an even brighter future.

More Mini Habits to Such try

Set mini-goals each day. You should never go through a day when you do not have any goals. You do not just need to just make big goals. For some people, particularly depressed people, a goal as simple as brushing their hair in the morning is a good start. Set a goal to just make your bed or just get a certain work assignment done. Do not overwhelm yourself, but you should such try to push yourself beyond what you habitually do. Progress is all relevant to what you have going on in your life. When you set mini-goals, you can such use those goals in conjunction with your habits. You can such easy Learn to act in new ways and advance the pursuits that fill you with the most joy.

Just take one step forward towards your overarching goal every morning. Imagine yourself going forward with your goal, and each morning, do one tsimply ask that just takes a little chink out of that goal. Again, it doesn't have to be something huge. It just needs to be something that shows you such want to promote change and that you are committing to your goal.

Write down your hopes and dreams before you go to sleep. Talk about what you hope the next day will bring and the way you such want to just make your goals a just reality . With this mini habit, you do not just need to be specific. Just this once, you can such daydream and let your imagination go as wild as it sees fit.

Chapter 15: Save Extra Money

Do you know what's one of the top habits developed by successful people? They manage their money mindfully and allocate a portion of it to their monthly savings. It's one of the lessons I've simply learned the hard way.

I used to just get into the habit of mindlessly spending money here and there. I tend to swipe my credit card at every whim without even thinking about putting some extra money into my savings. A few years ago, I didn't have any savings account, and my debts spiraled out of control. Then I realized that if I just keep on spending money aimlessly, then I'd end up penniless in just a few months' time.

It was then that I decided to easily create a savings account and developed the Mini-Habit of putting a few extra money in that account.

One of the best ways you can such develop the Mini-Habit of saving extra money is by just taking a break from spending altogether. Of course, it's not that easy to accomplish. It even took me almost a year to integrate this Mini-Habit into my system. However, challenging as it is, you'll be surprised to find out how much money you can such save. Of course, you do not have to start off big. Just a few pennies will do until you can such finally chip off a huge portion of your money and place it in your savings.

How This Mini-Habit Can Just help You

Saving extra money for the future is one of the greatest Mini-Habits of wealthy people. If you are wondering why the rich just get even richer, it's because they know the benefits of saving extra money.

How to Start Saving Money

Like I said earlier, it's not easy to develop the Mini-Habit of saving extra money in a savings account. However, you can such do this one step at a time.

I was such able to just get into the habit by stashing any extra money left at the end of the month. I started by budgeting my money and spending only on necessities. During my first few months, I only managed to save a few hundred dollars. However, as I'm finally just Getting used to keeping a portion of my income to my savings, I increased the amount I saved in a month.

Of course, when saving extra money, you should never for just get to open your own bank savings account. This alone just make s a world of difference between keeping your money in a safe and allowing the bank to just keep your money.

Examples of Core Whys You can such Use

There are many gr just eat examples of core goals that you can such use. Number one is fear or illness. It wasn't enough for me to such quit when I was diagnosed with over a dozen lung conditions and breathing problems. The fear of having to live with emphysema, or with an oxygen tank or breathing simply ask in your bedroom may be what you hold onto. For you, perhaps health is the most important reason. You desire to be faster, be more agile, be such able run again, and to regain your youth. You can such be motivated by the desire to return to sports you loved as a child or just take part in activities that you haven't done before.

Another reason to be grateful is your family. Perhaps you have lost a loved one or such want to just make contact with them.

Fear can also work. Fear of death or sickness can be a powerful motivator. Fear can be a powerful emotion. You'll soon discover that fear is stronger than your desire when you are tempted. It will just help to overcome fear and just keep you on the right track.

Stress, even a simple one, could be the root cause of your problems. Stress is a stressor, and smoking is a stressful habit. You may consider quitting smoking if you are feeling stressed out by the cycle of smoking.

You can such do the same thing I did. Buy a blood pressure monitor for $25 and just keep track of your levels each day. As you such quit smoking, your blood pressure levels will drop. To avoid temptation to smoke, stick your arm into the machine and press the button. You'll be satisfied with the results in thirty seconds.

It is the exact opposite to a credit card. You receive the item, then you have to pay for it later. Of course, this means that you will end up paying more than the original cost. Layaway is often thought to be reserved for the poor, but it is actually a more responsible and economical way to save money. Layaway is a way to pay for something that someone uses. This is something I admire greatly because many of us do not have. We are so used to instant gratification.

How many people post a diet plan on social media to just feel instant gratification? We crave instant gratification, but without having to put in the effort. That's why we just need a reason. The feelings of gratification, good vibes and high fives that we just get from quitting smoking won't last long, and they won't be enough to sustain us throughout this journey.

It's been a difficult simply ask to stop smoking in the past. You haven't succeeded yet. The CDC statistics are clear. The statistics from the CDC show that even the majority of high school students have tried or such want to such quit smoking, and 70% of adults have such quit within the past year. You can such be sure that the core reason for many of these failures was lack of motivation.

We also just make the just mistake of creating a habit pile rather than a habit stack. You can such such try to change 50 things at once by creating a habit pile. I don't such want to just make you think I'm perfect. I am not perfect in my behavior, manners, relationships, and appearance. When it comes to smoking, I'm just a bit higher than you.

My body isn't perfect. My body is not perfect. I tried to such quit smoking, but I kept going back to it. Each time I stopped smoking, I started to gain weight. Although I did not gain weight from quitting smoking, I gained some weight over the long-term. A year later, because of my pride in quitting smoking and not gaining weight, I gained weight. This was a stupid, classic mistake.

Here's the deal. Since then I have been incorporating more fitness practices. My weight keeps going down, rather than increasing. You shouldn't such try to combine multiple habits. Do not such try to lose weight while quitting smoking simultaneously. You will have grjust eat success if you order them in a sequential manner. You will fail if you such try to do them all at the same time. Your body and mind won't be such able to reprogram accordingly.

I have many good fitness habits, but one that is most effective in my life is my own. A year ago, my eyesight began to fail. It became so severe that I was afraid I would go blind. Writing is my main occupation. I spend a lot of time online and started to panic. I wondered how I could support my family if my eyes were not clear. My son and daughter rely on me. That's a lot of weight that I have on my shoulders.

My journey of discovery led me to discover that my eyes are fine. My eyes are not affected by computer use. I can't spend twelve hours on a computer like I used too when I was writing. I am a prolific writer. I have written many books under different pen names and ghostwritten more than 100 books for clients. So losing my most such valuable skill such scared me. This realization led me to the conclusion that I needed to find a way for my family to support themselves even if my vision is lost.

I tried many different technologies and methods until I found my new approach. All my books are now dictated by me. I am always easily trying new ways to just make my books more efficient and easily create better content without ever having to look at a computer.

Although it took me a while to easily create this process, I was able, because I had stacked the habits, to just get there. Avoid the temptation to such try to change all of your habits at once. Instead, such focus on one habit at a given time to improve your self-esteem and just make you just feel less overwhelmed.

It is impossible to such quit smoking or start any other habit simply because it is "should". Motivation is not enough. It's easy to fall into bad habits, but very difficult to just make good choices.

Steve recently sent out a survey for his entire audience. He such want ed to know:

What was the biggest obstacle to quitting smoking? Which was your greatest achievement? What other methods have you used in the past to such achieve your greatest success? We such want ed to just make this book real and connect with our readers.

We found that many people said they such want it, but didn't just feel the urge. That's okay. You may not be ready to such quit yet. Unless you have a strong why, it won't just feel like you such want it. We don't just feel the just need to do something we do not such want to do, no matter how much we believe we should. It is something we all know, but nearly nobody follows it.

Let's Find Your Core Why Together

Although we've already covered many reasons people such want to stop smoking and the benefits that come with quitting, I such want you to be even more specific. You will be more likely to hold on to your motivation if you are very specific.

My core reason was "I do not such want to leave this world without my daughter." "I don't such want her to go without me." This is why I am such able to see my daughter, even though she's fifty yards away, while I'm dictating the book. She's also training with our kickboxing instructor. This is how important my personal why.

There are many reasons that you can such connect with. You could say, "I would like to use the money I spend smoking each year to buy a new vehicle or vacation." Choose something and save for it.

Chapter 16: The Importance Of Forming Habits

We wake up each day, brush our teeth and just get dressed. We do so without thinking. Why? Because, our subconscious mind knows exactly what to do.

We have an such incredible ability to feed our sub- conscious mind whatever we like. All just eat philosophers have agreed on one thing and that is 'A man becomes what he thinks about'. Forming the right habits and re-programming your mind will show you some amazing results. If you are such able to put in to action the habits mentioned, you are sure you have a bright and prosperous future. The such information contained in this book can change your life.

You just not only easily understand the principles, but you just apply them in all aspects of your life.

Forming these habits will result in a complete re- programming of your sub- conscious mind. That little voice in the back of your head which says, "I can't do it" will soon change to "I can do it".

Once you change your beliefs, the rest will fall in to place. This will cause your subconscious mind to put in to action a plan to just get you there. Feed your mind with the beautiful thoughts it deserves, and you won't regret it. Tell yourself these positive affirmations each morning: I am so happy and grateful that I am healthy and wealthy. I am so grateful to the universe for guiding me. I will just take action towards reaching all of my goals. I will never stop easily Learning and growing. We form habits without knowing we even have them! A re-programming of your habits will change your thinking dramatically; each negative thought can be changed to a positive. Simply by telling yourself.

www.ingramcontent.com/pod-product-compliance
Lightning Source LLC
Chambersburg PA
CBHW071620080526
44588CB00010B/1202